Surround Me, Lord, With Color

St. John Paul II — an artist himself — kicked off his 1999 Letter to Artists with this familiar line from Genesis 1:31: "God saw all that he had made, and it was very good."

He did this, pointing to the very beginning of salvation history's tale, to draw the parallel that in our human desire for creativity, we inherently sense "some echo of the mystery of creation with which God, the sole creator of all things, has wished in some way to associate you."

Whether through growing families, daily labor, strengthening the Church, or simply through the use of colored pencils on paper, we as children of God have an innate desire to partake in God's creative nature.

It is our hope that this series of Adult Coloring Journals helps you tap into that desire to experience creativity with God. It is for this reason that we designed these not just as part of a recent fad but also as tools to draw you deeper into prayer and Scripture along with the very mystery of creation that God desires to share with you.

Now go create with God!

29 28 27 26 25 3 4 5 6 7 8 9

Our Sunday Visitor Publishing Division
Our Sunday Visitor, Inc.
200 Noll Plaza
Huntington, IN 46750
1-800-348-2440

ISBN: 978-1-68192-083-2 (Inventory No. T1825)
RELIGION/CHRISTIANITY/CATHOLIC

Cover design: Tyler Ottinger
Cover art: Shutterstock.com
Interior design: Tyler Ottinger

Interior art Shutterstock.com: OlichO, DT10, Guu, MOCHALOV GENNADII, image4stock, Olan, spinetta, Thoom, Farferros, BlueLotusArt, mashabr, Kate_bond, Kate_bond, Irina Simkina, Kate_bond, Julia Snegireva, Cerama_ama, Sarah Clark, IrinaKrivoruchko, karakotsya, OlichO, Maroshka, Julia Snegireva, Cerama_ama, Zetta, photo-nuke, oksanka007, Emila, Maroshka, oksanka007, IrinaKrivoruchko, IrinaKrivoruchko, oksanka007, Helen Lane, IrinaKrivoruchko, image4stock, ChaosMaker, Bourbon-88

PRINTED IN THE UNITED STATES OF AMERICA

A Prayer of St. Thomas Aquinas

Grant me grace, O merciful God,

"Perfection of moral virtue does not wholly take away the passions, but regulates them." — Thomas Aquinas

to desire ardently all that is pleasing to you,

to examine it prudently,

"If, then, you are looking for the way by which you should go, take Christ, because he himself is the way." — Thomas Aquinas

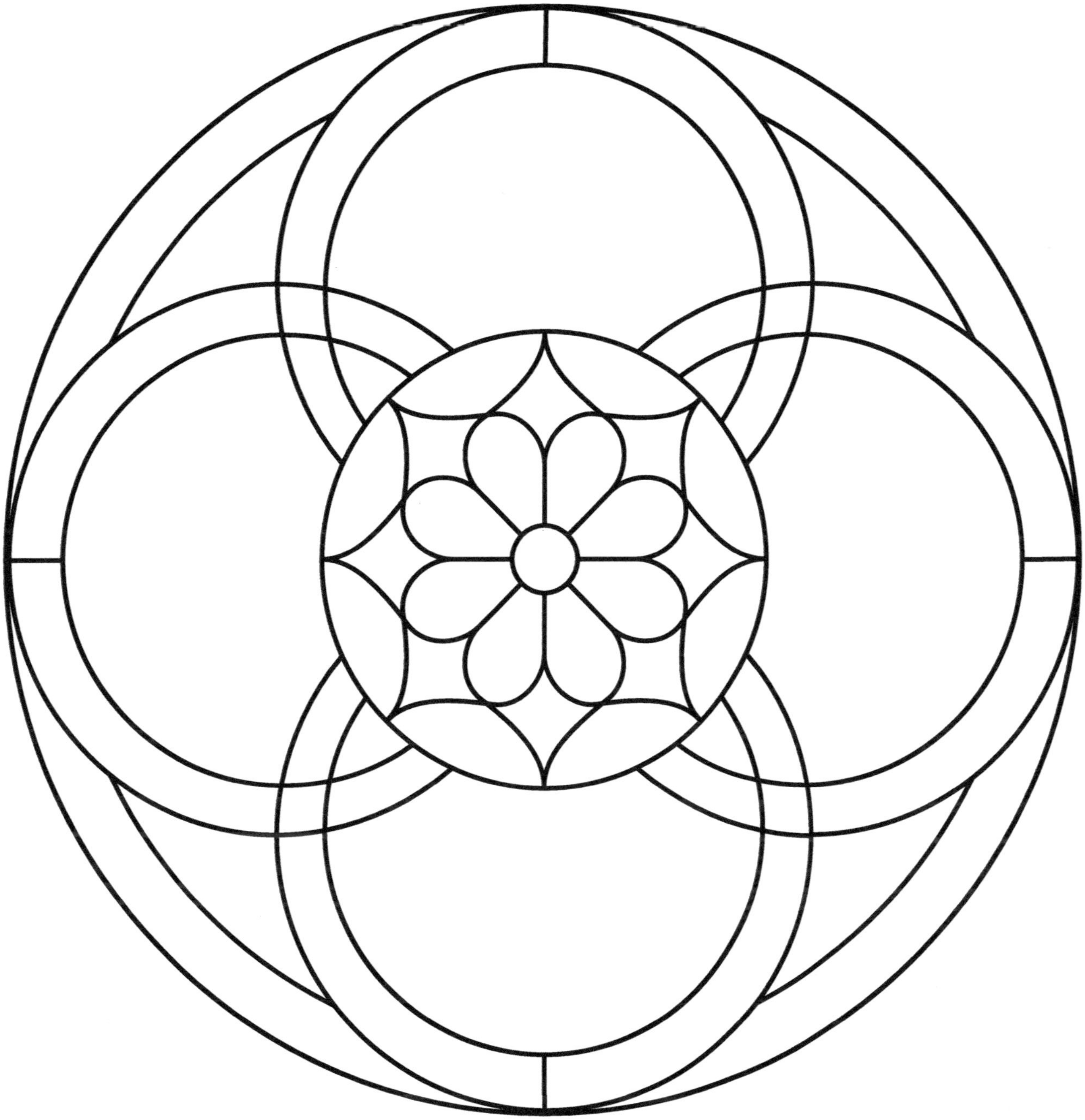

to acknowledge it truthfully,
and to accomplish it perfectly,

"Faith has to do with things that are not seen and hope with things that are not at hand." — Thomas Aquinas

for the praise and glory of your name.

Amen.

"Your heart's desire ... is your prayer; and if your desire continues uninterrupted, your prayer continues also.... The continuance of your longing is the continuance of your prayer." — St. Augustine

A Prayer of St. Augustine

Breathe in me, Holy Spirit, that all my thoughts may be holy.

"What does love look like? It has the hands to help others. It has the feet to hasten to the poor and needy. It has eyes to see misery and want. It has the ears to hear the sighs and sorrows of men. That is what love looks like." — St. Augustine

Act in me, Holy Spirit, that my work too may be holy.

"To fall in love with God is the greatest romance; to seek him the greatest adventure; to find him, the greatest human achievement." – attrib. St. Augustine

Draw my heart, Holy Spirit, that I may love only what is holy.

"Nothing whatever pertaining to godliness and real holiness can be accomplished without grace." — St. Augustine

Strengthen me, Holy Spirit, to defend all that is holy.

"O Holy Spirit, descend plentifully into my heart. Enlighten the dark corners of this neglected dwelling and scatter there thy cheerful beams." — St. Augustine

Guard me, Holy Spirit, that I may always be holy.

"If you are what you should be, you will set the whole world ablaze!"

— St. Catherine of Siena

For All the Saints

By WILLIAM W. HOW

"Lord, make me an instrument of your peace; where there is hatred, let me sow love; where there is injury, pardon; where there is doubt, faith; where there is despair, hope; where there is darkness, light; and where there is sadness, joy."

— St. Francis of Assisi

For all the saints who from their labors rest,
Who Thee by faith before the world confess,
Thy name, O Jesus, be forever blest,
Alleluia! Alleluia!

"Pray with great confidence, with confidence based upon the goodness and infinite generosity of God and upon the promises of Jesus Christ. God is a spring of living water which flows unceasingly into the hearts of those who pray."

— St. Louis de Montfort

Thou wast their Rock, their Fortress, and their Might;
Thou, Lord, their Captain in the well-fought fight;
Thou, in the darkness drear, their one true Light.
Alleluia! Alleluia!

"Pray, hope, and don't worry"

— St. Padre Pio

Oh, may Thy soldiers, faithful, true and bold,
Fight as the saints who nobly fought of old
And win with them the victor's crown of gold.
Alleluia! Alleluia!

"Ignorance of Scripture is ignorance of Christ."

— St. Jerome

O blest communion, fellowship divine,
We feebly struggle, they in glory shine;
Yet all are one in Thee, for all are Thine.
Alleluia! Alleluia!

"Teach us ... to give and not count the cost."

— St. Ignatius of Loyola

And when the fight is fierce, the warfare long,
Steals on the ear the distant triumph song,
And hearts are brave again, and arms are strong.
Alleluia! Alleluia!

"You have made us for yourself, O Lord, and our hearts are restless until they rest in you." — St. Augustine

But, lo, there breaks a yet more glorious day;
The saints triumphant rise in bright array;
The King of Glory passes on His way.
Alleluia! Alleluia!

"While you are proclaiming peace with your lips, be careful to have it even more fully in your heart." — St. Francis of Assisi

From earth's wide bounds, from ocean's farthest coast,
Through gates of pearl streams in the countless host,
Singing to Father, Son, and Holy Ghost,
Alleluia! Alleluia!

"You know well enough that our Lord does not look so much at the greatness of our actions, nor even at their difficulty, as at the love with which we do them."

— St. Thérèse of Lisieux

The golden evening brightens in the west;
Soon, soon, to faithful warriors cometh rest.
Sweet is the calm of Paradise the blest.
Alleluia! Alleluia!

"O Sacred Heart of Jesus, fountain of eternal life, your Heart is a glowing furnace of Love. You are my refuge and my sanctuary." — St. Gertrude the Great

Glory Be to Jesus

Trans. EDWARD CASWALL

"Whenever anything disagreeable or displeasing happens to you, remember Christ crucified and be silent." — St. John of the Cross

Glory be to Jesus,
Who in bitter pains
Poured for me the life-blood
From His sacred veins!

"Grace is nothing else than a certain beginning of glory in us."
— St. Thomas Aquinas

Grace and life eternal
In that blood I find,
Blest be His compassion,
Infinitely kind!

Prayer to the Sacred Heart of Jesus

O Heart of Love,
I put all my trust in you.
For I fear all things
from my own weakness,
but I hope for all things
from your goodness.
Amen.
— St. Margaret Mary Alacoque

Blest through endless ages
Be the precious stream
Which from endless torments
Did the world redeem!

"But above all preserve peace of heart. This is more valuable than any treasure. In order to preserve it there is nothing more useful than renouncing your own will and substituting for it the will of the divine heart. In this way his will can carry out for us whatever contributes to his glory, and we will be happy to be his subjects and to trust entirely in him." — St. Margaret Mary Alacoque

Abel's blood for vengeance
Pleaded to the skies,
But the blood of Jesus
For our pardon cries.

"The most deadly poison of our times is indifference.... And this happens, although the praise of God should know no limits.... Let us strive, therefore, to praise him to the greatest extent of our powers." — St. Maximilian Kolbe

Oft as earth exulting
Wafts its praise on high,
Angel hosts rejoicing
Make their glad reply.

"In all created things discern the providence and wisdom of God, and in all things give him thanks." — St. Teresa of Ávila

Lift we, then, our voices,
Swell the mighty flood,
Louder still and louder
Praise the precious blood!

"A liberal man will be enriched,
and one who waters will himself be watered."
— Proverbs 11:25

A Prayer for Generosity

Teach us, good Lord, to serve You as You deserve;

"He who has a bountiful eye will be blessed,
for he shares his bread with the poor."
— Proverbs 22:9

To give and not to count the cost;

"Give to the Most High as he has given,

and as generously as your hand has found."

— Sirach 35:10

To fight and not to heed the wounds;

"You will be enriched in every way for your great generosity, which through us will produce thanksgiving to God." — 2 Corinthians 9:11

To toil and not to seek for rest;

"The wicked borrows, and cannot pay back,

but the righteous is generous and gives."

— Psalm 37:21

To labor and not ask for any reward

"The fruit of the Spirit is love, joy, peace patience, kindness, goodness, faithfulness, gentleness, self-control." — Galatians 5:22

Save that of knowing that we do Your will.

ATTRIBUTED TO ST. IGNATIUS of LOYOLA

"For me prayer is a surge of the heart; it is a simple look turned toward heaven, it is a cry of recognition and of love, embracing both trial and joy."

— St. Thérèse of Lisieux

Serenity Prayer

God grant me serenity to accept the things
I cannot change,

"Prayer is the best armor we have, it is the key which opens the heart of God."

— St. Padre Pio

Courage to change the things I can,

"Life with Christ is a wonderful adventure."

— St. John Paul II

and

Wisdom to know the difference.

"Do not neglect to show hospitality to strangers, for thereby some have entertained angels unawares." — Hebrews 13:2

Prayer for Welcoming Guests

May grace be yours
and peace in abundance from God,
now and for ever.
Amen.

"Christ with me, Christ before me, Christ behind me, Christ within me, Christ beneath me, Christ above me." — St. Patrick

Irish Blessing

May the road rise up to meet you, may the wind be ever at your back.

"And he watched over me before I knew him and before I learned sense or even distinguished between good and evil." – St. Patrick

May the sun shine warm upon your face and
the rain fall softly on your fields.
And until we meet again, may God hold you in
the hollow of His hand.

"Be still and know that I am God.

Be still and know that I am.

Be still and know.

Be still.

Be."

– based on Psalm 46:10